Haiku for the Single Girl

Haiku for the Single Girl

Beth Griffenhagen

ILLUSTRATIONS BY

Cynthia Vehslage Meyers

PENGUIN BOOKS

PENGUIN BOOKS
Published by the Penguin Group
Penguin Group (USA) Inc.,
375 Hudson Street, New York, New York 10014, U.S.A.
Penguin Group (Canada), 90 Eglinton Avenue East, Suite 700, Toronto,
Ontario, Canada M4P 2Y3 (a division of Pearson Penguin Canada Inc.)
Penguin Books Ltd, 80 Strand, London WC2R 0RL, England
Penguin Ireland, 25 St Stephen's Green, Dublin 2,
Ireland (a division of Penguin Books Ltd)
Penguin Group (Australia), 250 Camberwell Road, Camberwell,
Victoria 3124, Australia (a division of Pearson Australia Group Pty Ltd)
Penguin Books India Pvt Ltd, 11 Community Centre,
Panchsheel Park, New Delhi - 110 017, India
Penguin Group (NZ), 67 Apollo Drive, Rosedale, Auckland 0632,
New Zealand (a division of Pearson New Zealand Ltd)
Penguin Books (South Africa) (Pty) Ltd, 24 Sturdee Avenue,
Rosebank, Johannesburg 2196, South Africa

Penguin Books Ltd, Registered Offices:
80 Strand, London WC2R 0RL, England

First published in Penguin Books 2011

1   3   5   7   9   10   8   6   4   2

LIBRARY OF CONGRESS CATALOGING IN PUBLICATION DATA
Griffenhagen, Beth.
Haiku for the single girl / Beth Griffenhagen ;
illustrations by Cynthia Vehslage Meyers.
p. cm.
ISBN 978-0-14-312001-8
1. Dating (Social customs)—Poetry. 2. Haiku, American.
I. Meyers, Cynthia Vehslage. II. Title.
PS3607.R543H35 2011
811'.6—dc22   2011026016

Printed in the United States of America

Haiku for the Single Girl

I feel its approach,

Inevitable as death:

Internet dating.

I walk home alone,

Bag covered in Cheeto dust.

Should this depress me?

My high school sweetheart

Has a toddler, and a gut,

But I'd take him back.

I am convinced that

All available men are

Somehow damaged goods.

This town is alive

With everything except

Eligible men.

I smile to myself

Because I have a secret:

My time is my own.

Halloween party;

I go as the Swedish Chef.

Note to self: not cute.

Sadly, the only

Guy I'm going steady with

Is my bartender.

What makes me nervous

Is the thought that I'll forget

How to date at all.

After a dry spell

It's impressive how quickly

Standards are lowered.

I now understand

The appeal of younger men,

Which makes me feel old.

"Whoa-oh here she comes,

Watch out boy, she'll chew you up!"

Eh, I've been called worse.

I always feel proud,

So why is it referred to

As the walk of shame?

Purchasing Plan B

At my local CVS.

Don't judge me, sales clerk!

If you're into her

Don't make her your Facebook friend.

Be a man, and text!

I try to avoid

Artistic communities.

(Throws off my gaydar.)

I hope that men will

Forgive me for not being

Zooey Deschanel.

Eyelash extensions?

Really? This is standard now?

Shit, man . . . I give up.

Whenever I spot

A cool pair of shoes, attached

Is an Asian chick.

I just bought makeup

That offers "more coverage."

The battle begins . . .

It turns out staring

Is a great way to seduce

(narcissistic) men.

Sure, I have "a type":

Tall, dark, and handsome with a

Peter Pan complex.

Spotted from afar

I give him the head to toe.

Oh! Fuck you, thumb ring.

Solitude causes

Loneliness, yes, but also

Fits of ecstasy.

When it's bad, you think,

I *could* be a lesbian.

Alas, oral sex.

Always, on the train

Babies stare at me, wide-eyed.

My ovaries hurt.

It would appear that

My biological clock

Has a snooze button.

At a friend's wedding,

Of course the biggest douche bag

Is hitting on me.

In my neighborhood

Even the homeless woman

Has a boyfriend. Sigh.

No more late night texts.

All my booty calls got bored.

Or worse, got girlfriends.

Some girls find ice cream

Therapeutic . . . I'll stick to

Drinking heavily.

Internet stalking . . .

Oh, sugar pie, honey bunch,

I can't help myself.

I saw an old flame

And he looked. Just. Terrible.

Ah, schadenfreude.

Sometimes I wonder

How different life would be

If I had cleavage.

A kiss on the hand

May be quite continental . . .

Buy me dinner first.

On my kitchen floor

We fucked loudly, more than once.

Take that, married friends!

He had a body

Like an underwear model,

So . . . I had no choice.

It was 4 a.m.

I saw him naked, eating,

And it felt like love.

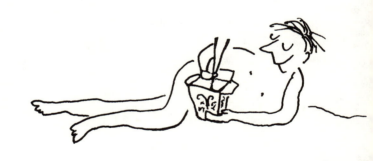

My mind's petals plucked

He loves me? He loves me not?

Ad infinitum.

The single girl's life

Is not a Cathy cartoon.

It's much funnier.

"Hemlines and haircuts."

Sure, but when did we decide

To stop wearing pants?

I thought with age came

If not a good man, good skin?

None of the above.

Some advice, ladies:

When you wear wedge heels and shorts

You just look like whores.

I can't get a date,

Yet I've been invited to

Multiple threesomes.

All of these young men,

Ironically mustachioed,

They bore me to tears.

the
SALVADOR
DALI

the
Poirot

the
EASY
RiDeR

Fleeting fetishes

Drift in and out of my life

Like guys on skateboards.

I like trysts with guys

From other countries. It's like

Stamping your passport!

"My bad," he mumbled

Right after he *came.* I thought,

"How did I get here?"

Construction workers:

Unfairly stereotyped?

I hear no catcalls.

From random street guy

The best pickup line ever:

"I'll make you breakfast!"

On the street I watch

Men leer at anything curved.

They're not that picky.

Aren't men ashamed

When they talk to their girlfriends

In that stupid voice?

I'm apathetic

About my chipped nail polish

Among other things.

Nerdy Jewish boys.

How did a Southern Baptist

Come to love you so?

Men don't realize

We women thrill to conquest

As much as they do.

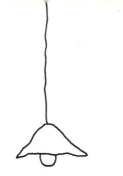

His proposition:

"Let's make out like teenagers!"

How could I refuse?

He said, "I love you"

During sex. Rookie mistake.

(I wish he'd meant it.)

Well, the good news is

If I settle down someday

I won't ask, "What if . . . ?"

Waiting by myself

In line for the taco truck

I look pathetic.

Eating sauerkraut

On the couch, straight from the jar . . .

This is my nadir.

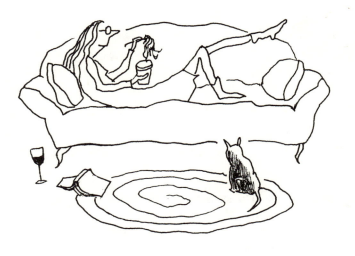

My neighbor enjoys

Sleeveless shirts AND owns a cat.

I should ask him out.

Bad breakup? Divorced?

Revisionist history:

Good for what ails ya!

Dear Future Husband,

Hope you like a.m. blow jobs

And pizza. Call me!

His shoulders are broad,

Like his smile. I think, maybe,

"This man could love me."

He makes me happy.

If he also makes me sad,

Then I'll know it's love.

It's worth noting here,

Beyoncé's "Single Ladies"

Was written by men.

Dating postdivorce . . .

The game's changed, the rules haven't.

Screw this, where's the wine?

My generation

Has a siren song. It goes:

"He's probably gay."

One night my mom asked,

"You do still like boys," (pause) "right?"

Yes, Mom. Sadly, yes.

Ironically,

"As long as you're happy" is

The saddest refrain.

As I get older,

I can hear all of my "whens"

Transform into "ifs."

I've thought about it,

And we all want the same thing:

Friends with benefits.

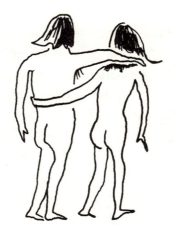

ACKNOWLEDGMENTS · *Beth*

Beth would like to thank:

The brave people of books: Stephanie Cabot and Chris Parris-Lamb at Gernert Co., and Stephen Morrison and Becca Hunt at Penguin. And perhaps the bravest of them all, Cynthia Meyers.

The original haiku fan club: Louise Geller, Martha Kaiser and Dan Sokoloff, Amelia Peláez Torres and Pedro Feria Pino, Whitney Parris-Lamb, Kate Elia, and Nicolle Feria Pino.

My besties: Ingrid Schwamb, Lis and Ethan Whittet, Rachel Sharpe May, and Megan Meagher.

My family, who taught me to celebrate weirdness and words: Mom, Dad, Mary, Jill, and Chris. And my grandmas, fellow single girls, Peggy Griffenhagen and Betty Butler.

ACKNOWLEDGMENTS · *Cynthia*

Cynthia would like to thank:

Stephanie Cabot, Chris Parris-Lamb, Stephen Morrison, and Becca Hunt, for your vision and imagination and wondrous leap of faith.

Beth Griffenhagen, for your crazy, beautiful mind!

Steve, Lily, and Nicky, for your love, support, and inspiration—and for letting me take over the kitchen table.

Creative collaborators: Amanda, Jessica, and Shira, for your tireless brainstorming and spot-on advice!

Personal advisers/contributors to this project: Laura, Soupie, Chris, Kelli, Helen, Pearson, Lisa, Eliot, Hildurg, Electra, Beth, Stacey, Sarah, Jessica, Justine, Andrea, Clare, Lanie, Steffi, Laurie, Diana, Kathleen, Michelle, Rachel, Laurie, Sarah, Sandrine, Jennifer, and Dick Pew.

And Mom and Dad, Rita and Bernie, Emmy and Stevie, for your steadfast, boundless enthusiasm for the scribbly line.

Beth Griffenhagen

Beth's a single girl

Living in New York City.

This is her first book.

Cynthia Vehslage Meyers

Cynthia Meyers

Lives and draws in Ridgefield, Conn.

She was once single.